Samantha liked to help.
She liked to build and fix things.

"Hey, Sam," said Dad. "I can't find my wrench.
Will you go to Uncle John's
and borrow one for me?"

"Sure," replied Sam.
"I like to go to Uncle John's."

"Please don't get sidetracked," said Dad.
"I really need that wrench."

"You can count on me," said Sam.

She climbed the fence and walked behind
two houses to Uncle John's house.

Uncle John was working
on his boat.

"Hi, Sam," said Uncle John.
"It's good to see you.
Will you hold this board for me
while I hammer in this nail?"

Sam held the board straight
and pushed on it so it wouldn't
move when the nail went in.

"These nails are not quite long enough," said Uncle John. "Would you mind going over to Mr. Nelson's to borrow a few longer ones?"

"OK," said Sam.

"Please don't get sidetracked," said Uncle John. "I really need those nails."

"You can count on me," said Sam.

She skipped down to the house at the end of the block. Mr. Nelson's two dogs jumped up to greet her as she unlatched the gate.

Mr. Nelson was painting the fence.

"Hi, Sam," said Mr. Nelson.
"I haven't seen you in a long time.
Would you like to help?" he asked,
pointing to the painting supplies.

Samantha put on a big, old shirt
and dipped a brush in the paint.
She made long strokes up and down.
She made long strokes from
side to side.

"There are a few loose boards in this fence," said Mr. Nelson. "I'd like to fix them but I can't find my hammer. Would you mind going over to Mrs. Green's to borrow her hammer?" he asked.

"Not at all," said Sam. "She has a great backyard."

"Now don't get sidetracked," said Mr. Nelson. "I really need that hammer."

"You can count on me," said Sam.

Sam ran all the way down the hill behind Mr. Nelson's house.
She took a shortcut through the playground.
She swung across the monkey bars, two bars at a time.

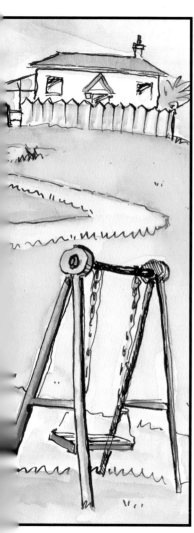

She found Mrs. Green watering her vegetable garden.
A scarecrow stood in the center of the garden.
Corks dangled from his hat.

"Hi, Sam," said Mrs. Green.
"My, look how you've grown."

"Hi, Mrs. Green," said Sam.
"That's a terrific scarecrow!"

"Would you water the tomato plants
for me, Sam?" asked Mrs. Green,
handing Sam the hose.
"I just need to put some stakes
in the ground to mark
what I've planted," she said.

Sam watered around the roots. She was
careful not to knock any flowers off
the plants with the spray of water.

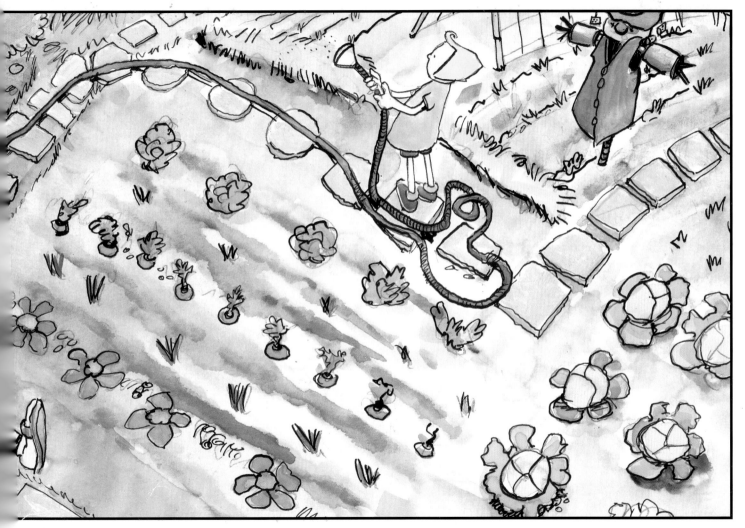

Mrs. Green hammered stakes
up and down the rows.

"I just remembered," she said.
"I think I borrowed this hammer
from Mr. Nelson and
forgot to return it to him.
Would you mind dropping it
by his house on your way home?"
she asked as she turned off
the tap.

Sam took the shortcut through the playground on her way back. She climbed the steps of the slide and went down one time.

She climbed the hill behind Mr. Nelson's house by walking backward. It was easier that way.

"Thank you, Sam," said Mr. Nelson when Sam gave him the hammer. "You're a great kid."

Sam told him about the scarecrow as Mr. Nelson pulled old nails from the fence and hammered in new ones.

"This reminds me," said Mr. Nelson. "I owe your Uncle John some long nails, and I just bought a new, full box. Would you mind dropping these off at his house on your way home?" he asked as he put some in a paper sack.

All the way to Uncle John's house,
Sam pretended to walk a tightrope down the sidewalk.

Uncle John was tightening nuts and bolts on his boat.

"Good job, Sam," said Uncle John, taking the sack of nails. "I only have a few more nuts and bolts to tighten and she'll be ready to take out this weekend. Do you want to go with me?" he asked.

"Sure!" said Sam. "I'll ask Dad if it's OK."

"By the way, will you give him this wrench for me, Sam?" asked Uncle John. "He loaned it to me weeks ago."

Sam crossed behind two houses and peeked over the fence.

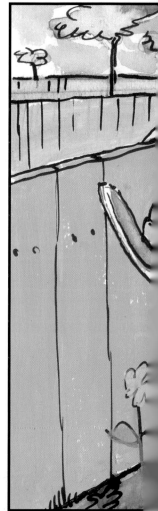

Dad was working under the hood of the car.

"I'm back, Dad," said Sam.

Dad took the wrench from Sam and helped her climb over the fence.

"That's my girl!" said Dad. "And you didn't even get sidetracked."

"Well, Dad," said Sam,
"you know you can count on me."

"Yes, Sam," said Dad, "I know I can."